Make the Grade!

TESTS

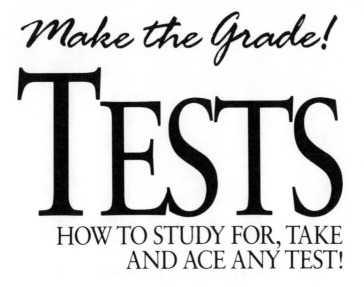

Make the Grade!

TESTS

HOW TO STUDY FOR, TAKE AND ACE ANY TEST!

E. RICHARD CHURCHILL

PRICE STERN SLOAN
Los Angeles

© 1989 by Tern Enterprises, Inc.

Published by Price Stern Sloan, Inc.
360 North La Cienega Boulevard,
Los Angeles, California 90048

Printed in the United States of America.
9 8 7 6 5 4 3 2 1

Cover and interior design by Victor Mazurkiewicz

Library of Congress Cataloging-in-Publication Data

Churchill, E. Richard (Elmer Richard)
    Tests.

    (Make the grade)
    Includes index.
    Summary: A reference guide for junior and senior high school students on how to develop study skills to be able to score higher on tests.
    $4.95
    1. Test-taking skills—Juvenile literature.
2. Study, Method of—Juvenile literature. [1. Test-taking skills. 2. Study, Method of] I. Title. II. Series.
LB3060.57.C48   1989   371.3'028'12   89-3500
ISBN: 0-89586-774-5

——— Table of Contents ———

How Can This Book Help Me?

Right now you may be asking yourself, "Why do I need this book?" We will discuss how this book can help you in a few moments. First, why not answer a few questions about your test-taking ability? Write "yes" or "no" in the space before each question.

---

1. ___ Did you get a perfect score on each of the last ten tests you took?
2. ___ Do you always get ready to take a test feeling confident and totally prepared?
3. ___ Do you sometimes read a test question and have little or no idea what the answer should be?
4. ___ Are you ever nervous or fearful when your teacher is handing out the test you are about to take?
5. ___ Have you ever come to class completely unprepared for a test?
6. ___ Have you sometimes finished a test and promised yourself that next time you'd be better prepared?

Did you answer "no" to either of the first two questions? Did you answer "yes" to any of the other four? If so, you need to modify, or even transform completely, the way you deal with tests.

The primary purpose of this book is to help you get over any fear of tests that you might have. It will also show you how to prepare for tests so you are always ready for whatever your teachers have in store — from pop quizzes to long essay tests. Getting the upper hand where tests are concerned makes learning a lot more enjoyable, and goes a long way toward building your self-confidence, too. It's that sense of "test mastery" that this book is meant to instill in anyone who follows its suggestions and advice.

At this point we can be reasonably sure of two things: First, unless you are a total genius, you can use a bit of help (and maybe a lot of help) in learning how to prepare for and take tests.

Second, you just about have to agree that anything which will improve your test-taking ability is going to make things easier for you.

Now that you have an idea how this book can help you, let's get the show on the road.

CHAPTER 1

What Can Keep Me from Acing My Tests?

O ur first step in learning how to do better when taking tests is to examine the many things which make it difficult or even impossible to do well.

Failure to Read Assignments Makes Tests Impossible

Let's take another quick quiz. Fill in the blank spaces in each statement with the word or date which makes the statement correct.

---

1. In 1914, Sarajevo was the capital of _____.
2. On _____, 1914, Archduke Francis Ferdinand was shot and killed by an assassin.
3. The leaders of Austria-Hungary blamed the nation of _____ for the murder of the archduke.

Say what? How can you be expected to answer questions about the beginning of World War I when you haven't read the material? That's precisely the problem. *How can you answer any test question without first reading the assignment?* And yet, every day students (hopefully not you) face tests covering material they have not studied. Perhaps they forgot to do the appropriate assignment. Or perhaps they forgot the test was going to be given so soon. Whatever the reasons, remember there are no *excuses* for this happening. The most basic way to even begin thinking about test mastery is to first read the assigned lesson. (In case you're interested, the answers to the test above are Bosnia, June 18 and Serbia.)

Learn to Listen in Class or Be Ready to Fail Some Tests

No one knows better than your teacher that it is difficult for students to pay attention every second of every class period. That's why most teachers repeat important points and try to approach information they want to stress in several different ways.

Keep in mind, too, that you are not going to fail a test just because you happen to spend thirty seconds thinking about what you are going to do next weekend or because you found some member of the opposite sex more interesting than what your teacher was saying. However, you can't spend half of every class period thinking about such things. Not, that is, if you have any hope of knowing what the classes were all about.

One good way to make sure you are really listening — and not just letting the teacher's words flow past you like ducks swimming in a pond — is to take notes. We'll discuss note taking in detail later on. For now, try to get in the habit of jotting down important ideas which come up during class discussion.

If You Don't Understand, Ask Questions

It's hard for some students to put up their hands and ask questions in class. But unless you ask questions about things you don't understand, the teacher is likely to go on to another topic and assume you did understand. Later, when those things appear on a test, is a poor time to complain, "I didn't understand this when we talked about it two weeks ago." If you were the teacher, would you be sympathetic to such a line?

Worse than not understanding an important point is not understanding when things which follow are based on that one idea or fact. This can be especially disastrous in math class. Sara didn't understand what her teacher meant when he told the class, "When adding or subtracting decimal fractions, be sure to align the decimal points." Sara should have asked what was meant by "align," but she kept quiet because she didn't want her friends to think she was stupid. Before she knew it, the class was adding and subtracting tenths, hundredths and thousandths, all in the same problem. The next day she failed a surprise quiz on decimals and still didn't know what "align the decimal points" meant.

Try to keep in mind that there is no such thing as a dumb question if you are asking it to understand better. If you are shy about speaking up in class, just concentrate on the teacher and ask your question. Which would you rather do: force yourself to ask a question or get a poor grade?

It's Hard to Learn When You Miss Class

Sometimes missing class can't be helped. For one thing, no matter how hard we try to stay healthy, most of us are bound to get sick once in a while. But is being ill the only valid reason for missing class? Are there other good reasons students don't attend every class every day of the school year? Mark with an "x" any of the following situations you think reasonably warrant being absent from class.

1. ___A family member has died and the funeral is on a school day.
2. ___ Dad or Mom just got paid and you want to shop for new clothing and new shoes.
3. ___ Your folks are going to London for two weeks and want to take you with them.
4. ___ You are in the big variety show and rehearsal is during school time.
5. ___ It is spring and Mr. Colman doesn't really care whether you come to his Friday afternoon class or not.

You doubtlessly considered the first reason valid. The second idea is not a good reason for missing school, but you'd be amazed how many students and their parents consider a trip to the mall a substitute for attending class. How about the third reason? If your teacher looks shocked and exclaims, "Two weeks! You can't miss that much school!" then you have a problem. The teacher who says, "What an opportunity! Leave your books at home and spend your time learning" is probably one of the best you'll ever have. The fourth reason is valid, too; teachers understand that sometimes school commitments conflict with each other. If you marked the last idea, well, you must have misread the question.

Not all teachers make a big deal about your skipping class, but, like Santa Claus and "Big Brother," they're aware. Mr. Cristman was one of those teachers. He taught civics and government. Every Friday afternoon one spring, three or four of the hero athletes (we called them jocks) cut his class. Mr. Cristman never complained and never reported them to the principal. But one Friday he gave the class a lot of notes and said, "These are important. Better learn them." The next test was a five-question essay extravaganza. Guess where all five questions came from. Guess which three or four fellows turned in blank test papers.

One good way to cover yourself for any absences is to make a deal with a classmate early on in the term: If one of you is absent, the other will take extra good notes and then share them. Make sure any new assignments or tests are included in the notes. And if you know you're going to miss several days of school, you might want to ask your note-taking friend or friends to drop the notes off at your home (providing, of course, you are well enough to do a bit of work while you're out of school).

Forgetting Is a Real Problem for Some Students

Pretend you are a teacher. Which of the following excuses would you be likely to accept?

1. ___ We have a test today? I forgot all about it, so may I take it tomorrow?
2. ___ I didn't do my homework because I forgot what our assignment was. Is it okay if I hand it in later?
3. ___ Hello, Mrs. White. I'm sorry to call you at midnight but I forgot what pages you told us to read for discussion tomorrow.
4. ___ I can't remember all those names you had on the board yesterday. Would you put them up again so I can study them during class?

If you marked any of the excuses as reasonable you have a lot to learn about the care and understanding of teachers!

How can you avoid forgetting? *Write things down.* Notes give you something to look back at, and *the very act of writing the note helps you remember,* too. What if you forget to write down an assignment so you won't forget it? In that case your teacher will probably "forget" to give you a good grade.

All kidding aside, a certain amount of discipline is required. Once you get into the habit, writing down assignments, important ideas and the like will become a natural part of the way you operate.

If You Don't Follow Test Directions, Things Can Get Real Bad

One reason some students do poorly on tests is their failure to follow directions. These directions may be written on the test or spoken aloud by the teacher. Whichever the case, if you don't follow directions, you may end up in big trouble. So why don't all students follow all directions all the time?

Perhaps Lauren asked you to pick up her pencil just as Mr. Wilson was telling you to be sure to give the first and last name of every person whose name you used on the history test. Maybe Mr. Wilson was giving oral instructions while he handed out the papers but instead of listening you were already looking at your test. Or it could be that this was one of those times that Tom and Joe wandered in late and were clowning around, diverting your attention.

Whatever the case, you've got to listen to directions. If you don't understand those directions, ask for a replay. This is just as important as asking for an explanation in class. The same is true of written directions, which may also leave you wondering. When this happens, take a few seconds and reread them. If still in doubt, ask. The time to admit you don't understand is *before* you start the test, not days later when you are looking at your returned test and thinking that all the red check marks remind you of a bad case of measles. Of course, you can always tell your teacher, "I'm sorry I didn't follow directions. May I retake the test?" That excuse and two quarters will get you a soda — and not much more.

Misread Test Questions Are Hard to Answer Correctly

Why do students misread test questions? Sometimes just the excitement of taking a test will cause difficulties with reading questions. Other times a student has one thing in mind and fails to realize the question says something else entirely.

Here's an example which cost a point on a science test many years ago but has never been forgotten. The question read: What percentage of the atmosphere is composed of carbon dioxide? The student (me, who else?) read "carbon *mon*oxide" instead and answered accordingly. To make matters worse, the student (yours truly) then got bent out of shape at the check mark and loudly informed the teacher that a mistake had been made in grading. You can imagine the student, the teacher and the rest of the class if you like. I'd rather not; the memory is still too painful.

By now you should have a pretty good idea of all the things which can keep you from doing well on a test. Next we'll discover what you can do to *improve* your ability to take tests.

TEST-TAKING TIPS

- Read all assignments if you want to understand.
- Listen in class to ensure success.
- Ask that question now!
- Consistent attendance is half the battle.
- Don't rely on memory — *write things down*!

CHAPTER 2

How Can I Best Prepare for a Test?

There are a number of things students can do to prepare for a test. Some ideas work better for one person than for another, and a few ideas work well for all students.

In this chapter we will look at plans of attack which are successful for most students. As you read you will probably have ideas which will make a plan better for you. That's great! Feel free to add to any study plan so that it works for you.

Come to Class Prepared

Since preparing for a test begins with preparing for class, make it a habit to come prepared to class every single day. What exactly does this involve? Take a look at the ideas below and mark with an "x" each one you think is part of coming to class properly prepared.

1. ___ Be sure you have note paper and a pencil or pen.
2. ___ If your class has a text (most do, and each textbook seems bigger than the one used the previous year), bring the text to class each day.
3. ___ Make certain your supply of candy and gum will last through the class session.
4. ___ If you have an assignment due, make sure you have it with you. (It goes without saying it should be finished!)

11

5. ___Bring along your class notes from previous classes to refer to if necessary.
6. ___Have your comb, lip-gloss and other such items with you so you can look your best.
7. ___Come ready to listen, take part and learn.

You probably did not mark item three or six, but if not, why not? Just kidding. The truth is that too many students spend little time paying attention and more time trying to avoid getting caught eating candy and gum or participating in other forms of nonsense. More to the point, many students slip all too easily into the habit of bringing things to class which distract them from the learning at hand. Take a few seconds to make a mental list of those things you carry to any given class. Surprised at what you came up with? In the future, leave the auto magazines, the beauty paraphernalia and the pocketful of rubber bands at home, or at least in your locker.

Keep a List of Assignments Which Are Due

Earlier we talked about making a note of those things which must be remembered. Now we want to go one step further — we want to keep a written assignment list such as the one below. With so many classes and so many extracurricular activities, it can become extremely easy to forget assignments, especially shorter ones that may be given on a day-to-day basis. But if you always make a note of such assignments, and then remember to check your assignment list, you won't get caught short. Such a chart takes about a minute to make and is well worth the effort.

Class	*Assignment*	*Date Due*

This simple chart does all that is necessary. A quick glance tells you what is due and when. Once you finish an assignment you can cross it off and go on to the next one.

Some students keep two kinds of assignment charts. The one above is perfect for daily assignments, but what about those big projects which may have several parts, each of them due at a different time? With major projects it is extremely easy to miss a due date unless you write down each part of the assignment and the appropriate deadline. A major report for English is a good example of such a project. The chart on the following page shows how this might be plotted out. Check it daily to make certain you keep in mind where you stand.

ENGLISH REPORT

Assignment	Date Due
Topic Chosen	Jan. 10
List of Potential References	Jan. 17
Outline	Jan. 20
Note Cards Finished for Checking	Feb. 7
Note Cards Numbered and Assigned to Outline	Feb. 10
First Draft Complete	Feb. 18
Bibliography Finished and in for Checking	Feb. 21
Final Draft Complete, Bibliography, Title Page, and Cover	Feb. 25

It takes only a few seconds to record assignments, and once you do you won't forget them. It's virtually that simple.

How do tests fit in to an assignment chart? Think of an upcoming test as a special assignment and record that date as soon as it is scheduled. You may even want a special assignment page for test dates or a calendar that will help you visualize your due dates. That's entirely up to you. The important thing is to get into the habit of writing things down on the list because it's an easy way to make certain you are prepared.

Get into the Study Mode

We've all read the story of Abraham Lincoln and his efforts to study and learn on his own. As you recall, Abe studied before the fireplace at night and used a piece of charcoal to write on an old shingle — not exactly the kind of situation in which most of us would do our best work. However, Abe's poor study conditions do illustrate one big truth: *Those who really want to learn will find a place and a way to study no matter how bad things are.*

Students can and do study in noisy or crowded locations. They hit the books in poorly lighted areas, may shiver when the heat goes off at night and endure any number of uncomfortable situations and conditions. The fact is, we do what we have to do and make the best of it. Still, there are some basic things about study areas which are worth discussing. The closer you come to having a perfect study area the more likely you are to find it easy to prepare for those tests which always seem just around the corner.

Do we need to mention that a fairly quiet place is usually considered a good beginning for a study area? This pretty much rules out having the radio or stereo cranked up to the max as you try to make sense of your English assignment.

You need plenty of light so you can read your books and notes easily, and enough pencils, pens, and paper to see you through your study session.

A desk or table large enough to hold all your materials really helps. There's something exciting, too, about having everything laid out in front of you as you work.

It's also great to have a comfortable chair (but not too comfortable, or you'll find yourself dozing off right in the middle of the Civil War!).

Here's a tip for getting into the proper mode and mood to study. Gather all the materials you need for your assignments. Sharpen your pencils and that sort of thing first so you aren't tempted to keep jumping up to do something you should have done before you sat down to work. If you want something to eat or drink, plan ahead so you have it ready to go. Better yet, use food and drink as a goal or reward by telling yourself, "When I finish my math assignment I'll pour myself a soda." Or, "When my English essay is finished I'll have that piece of cake that's been tempting me all evening."

Naturally, having your own quiet room is an ideal study situation, though the truth is we live in an imperfect world. Some students have a nearly perfect place in which to study, while others can't find a quiet, well-lighted spot to save their lives. But, somehow, all who want to study manage to accomplish the task. Since it is pretty close to impossible for most students to ace tests without studying, those who want to get test taking under control are going to have to learn to study in the places available to them — good, bad or indifferent. You can and will survive. Think of good old Abe Lincoln and his charcoal and shingle! *That* was a really poor study situation.

Just for the fun of it, rate the following study situations as either good, bad or questionable. Use the letters "G," "B" and "Q" if you wish.

---

1. ____ Your social studies teacher gives the class the last ten minutes of the period to begin reading the next lesson.
2. ____ Three of your best friends invite you over to study and watch a little television.
3. ____ You are baby-sitting for three little kids who are playing in the game room.
4. ____ The girl or guy you've had your eye on for a while suggests the two of you spend the evening at the public library.
5. ____ Your family members are all out of the house, leaving it as quiet as a tomb.
6. ____ When things get quiet at the fast-food spot where you work evenings you can sometimes find time to puzzle out a problem or two.
7. ____ Even though you have your own room, the sounds of your family having fun are easy to hear.

By now you should have realized that there is really no correct answer to most of these questions. Some people can study with their boy- or girlfriend at the library; others can't. Many students learn to study while parents and family argue or party or watch TV; some can't manage it. And if you feel that starting a reading assignment in the stillness of a classroom is a good time to get a jump on your homework, you should probably review what you already read as you continue to read it at home. Find the best place you can in which to study, prepare as well as possible, then concentrate on what you are doing. Remember: Most things take practice, so you can learn to study under poor conditions if you must. It just takes less effort when everything is ideal.

Pick the Best Time to Study

When is the best *time* to study? Certainly, if you make your study time quality time, if you really get down and dig, any time you study is the best time. Let's consider the question a little further to see if there really is a "best" time.

Many students find that hitting the books as soon as they get home from school — while things are still fresh in their minds — works best for them. Though they are tired from a day at school, they are a lot more alert than will be the case several hours later. Also, students who study early know they will have the rest of the evening to spend as they wish. This sort of goal or reward helps urge them on.

But, you're probably asking, what about sports practice, drama rehearsal, the school newspaper or after-school jobs? These activities are just as important in their own way as are study sessions. Obviously, if you have activities from the time school ends until dinnertime, you have to find another study time.

What about right after the evening meal? Many

find this the best time to begin homework. You're not hungry, so your stomach doesn't keep suggesting a break. It isn't so late you're likely to fall asleep at your desk. And unless your teachers have really piled it on, you have a fighting chance of finishing in time to watch your favorite TV program.

What about TV and studying? If your parents have made a "no TV until you finish all your homework" rule, the question is already answered. For most students, however, it is possible to budget their time so they can take a break and watch a program on the tube; this can be a reward for getting one assignment done by a certain time. (Please, please don't tell your parents that the book you are reading about mastering tests says you have to be allowed to watch TV every night. Life is hard enough without having your folks mad at me!)

Do we even need to say that it is a poor idea to watch the tube from seven until ten and then open your books for the first time? Some things are pretty obviously not going to work well, and this is one of them. How about setting your alarm and getting up in the early hours each morning? Speaking for myself, this just never worked. For one thing, getting up in the dark and trying to convince myself to study was a real pain. For another, what happens if you discover an assignment you thought would take half an hour becomes a mind-bender and takes an hour (or even more)? At night you can extend your time and battle a long assignment until you get the better of it. In the morning you have to get to school whether you have finished or not.

No matter when you study, give it your best shot. If you can set the same time each day (or most days), it helps establish a habit. Your mind begins to get geared up to study, and things go easier. Don't think you have to turn into a bookworm. Sports, clubs and work are important. The trick is to use your study time so well that you have time for other things.

Note Taking May Not Thrill You, but It's a Great Way to Remember

All sorts of people talk about taking notes, but very few ever explain how to take them. As we've already mentioned, the actual act of writing a note helps you remember. This is called a *memory aid* or a *mnemonic device.* Notes help you remember major points, and are great study aids around test time. No student should be without them. But how do you know what to write in your notes?

Notes should include important names, dates and events from history. They should include formulas and special processes in math. In English, notes may cover proper usage, special vocabulary meanings, ideas for better writing and the like. In short, a note is a brief reminder of anything important enough you need to remember it. You can jot down notes while listening to your teacher and while reading an assignment. The main idea is to include enough in each note so you can instantly recall what you need to know. *Don't make a note so long it stops being a note and becomes a paragraph.* Notes need not be sentences; phrases or just names and dates can serve perfectly well.

The best way to help you see how to take notes is to give some examples, both good and bad. Study the samples below. If the sample is too short to tell you what you need to know, mark it "S." If it is too long to be quickly read, mark it "L." Those samples which seem the proper length should be marked "R" for just right.

1. ___ George Washington — Continental Congress
2. ___ Washington, crossed Delaware Christmas night, surprised the Hessians at Trenton
3. ___ English, Philadelphia
4. ___ Saratoga proved to be the turning point in the Revolutionary War because the victory convinced the French to enter into a treaty with the Americans.
5. ___ Burgoyne surrendered October 17, 1777 at Saratoga.

See? You already know quite a bit about note taking. Obviously, the first and third examples are too short. The student knew what each meant when they were written, but how about two weeks later, with the midterm test fast approaching? Not a clue. Number four isn't a note; it's the sort of sentence you might write in a report. If every note were as long as this one, you'd never get your notes taken, much less, reviewed. Notes two and five tell enough to be useful yet are brief enough to be written and read quickly.

Make a habit of taking notes and you'll find it helps prepare for those dreaded tests. Because note taking requires practice, the time to begin is now. Don't get discouraged if you can't write down everything you hear or read. Just work at picking important points and noting them in short form. Pretty soon you'll develop a real skill and perhaps even your own form of shorthand. If your handwriting is sloppy or if you want to expand on your class notes, rewriting your notes at home is often useful.

Often your teacher gives clues as to what you should include in notes. When he or she says, "An important idea...This was a major factor...In summary...To conclude..." you have a good idea that whatever follows is important.

Another important tip: *Date your notes.* This is especially useful for loose-leaf paper that gets removed from a binder, it serves as a reference when studying in a group situation and it really helps when studying for the final exam and you want an overview of the class.

Plan Ahead to Study for Tests

Preparing for tests does not just happen; it is a planned activity. Once a test is announced and you have recorded that date on your assignment sheet, it's time to map out your plan of attack. There are several things to be done:

First and foremost, be absolutely positive you have read all the assignments the test will cover. Make certain you have taken enough notes to cover all the important points. Pay special attention in class and take notes when your teacher discusses material to be covered on the upcoming test.

Then, at least four days before the test, begin your actual study and review. Take some time to glance back over your reading assignments. Don't attempt to reread them but instead read the boldface headings, glance at pictures and their captions and read completely any chapter or unit summaries.

Begin the following day's study session by reviewing your notes. Once this is done it's time to get down to doing some bare-bones studying. There are a variety of successful study devices you should consider. We'll go over these in the following pages.

With the test only two days away, take time to review your notes again. Once this is accomplished, attempt to recall important facts, names, dates and ideas likely to be on the test. Then devote the remainder of this session to the study methods you find most helpful from among those presented in the pages ahead.

On the day before the test, glance over your reading assignments again and review your notes one last time. If you have prepared flash cards as suggested in the next section, go through them once more. Spend a few minutes with vocabulary lists or definitions you may have assembled, and quickly go over any other special devices you are using.

When test day dawns you can face the dreaded exam knowing your planning is about to pay off.

Now let's consider some study devices which have proven successful for many students.

Seeing Is Believing...and Recalling

Flash cards used to be familiar to all arithmetic students. Teachers used these cards to aid students in recalling instantly the answers to arithmetic combinations. But since teaching methods and tools change over the years, you may never have used flash cards. This is how they work:

One side of an arithmetic flash card presents a problem or number statement. The back of that card gives the correct answer. For example:

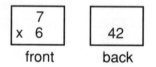

The teacher quickly holds up the card so you see the front in a flash. Then, also quick as a flash, you call out the answer.

So what do flash cards used for younger kids have to do with studying for the science test? Robert really enjoyed arithmetic flash cards in elementary school. When he began to study for science and history tests in junior high he devised his own flash cards to suit his now more sophisticated needs. For instance, in ninth grade he had to learn some of the symbols for the various elements in the Periodic Table, and constructed a set of simple flash cards out on note cards which looked like this:

He glanced at the front of the card, read the word "gold," then tried to recall the chemical symbol for gold, which is "Au." After either success or failure, Robert turned the card over, checked the answer, then went to the next card. Once he ran through the entire set of flash cards, Robert shuffled the pack and started over again. By changing the order of the cards he never fell into the trap of remembering one element because it always followed another.

For his history studying Robert set up flash cards in the same manner:

cotton gin	Eli Whitney, 1793

Missouri Compromise	Henry Clay Compromise of 1820 Maine free, Missouri slave No slaves Louisiana purchase

Robert's cards were as simple or as complex as necessary in order to help him study. These flash cards worked so well for Robert he kept on making them through high school and right on into college. In fact, he graduated with honors in engineering and is now making a handsome salary as a chemical engineer.

Another excellent study device similar to flash cards is an *information chart*. Depending upon the subject you are studying, your information chart may be simple or quite complicated. Here's part of one such chart a student made to help her review for a test on rocks and minerals:

GRANITE
Does not fizz in acid
Contains feldspar, quartz, biotite, hornblende
Igneous — often light colored but not always

OBSIDIAN
Does not fizz in acid
Content is glass
Natural glass formed when flowing lava cooled
  quickly
Black in color

PUMICE
Does not fizz in acid

Another variation, a *time chart*, can provide a quick way to check historical facts and enable you to keep in mind the order in which events occurred. Such a chart for reviewing the Spanish-American War might begin like this:

1819   Florida became part of the U.S.
1823   Monroe Doctrine prevented Spain from
       regaining colonies in Latin America
1854   U.S. attempted to purchase Cuba
1873   Ten Years' War began
1895   Uprisings all over Cuba

The idea which makes flash cards and information and time charts good study devices is simple: They enable the student to select *which* material to study, and they summarize that material in a manner which is easy to review. Also, rewriting and transferring the information from your notes to a card or chart is another mnemonic device!

Let Your Teacher Clue You In

Ask your teacher what will be on a test, even if he or she does not volunteer the information. It's no time to be shy when your grade is at stake. *Not only do you want to know exactly what material will be covered, you need to know what type of test you will be taking.* If you are going to have an essay test you'll want to study with broad topics in mind. Objective tests such as true/false and completion (or fill-in) require you to study details. Knowing what form the test will take gives you an edge in studying. (We'll talk about how to take each type of test later in this book.)

Teachers give hints as to what will be tested by the way they teach class. Pay careful attention to what points and ideas your teacher stresses during daily class meetings. A name, date, process or fact which your teacher keeps mentioning is almost certain to appear on a test.

If you have a "test-prep" question-and-answer session don't be afraid to ask questions about any points of which you are not certain. Then really listen to the answers — to your question and to those posed by others. Even though many students look at question-and-answer sessions as a great way to use up class time without actually *doing* anything, they are actually a fine opportunity to allow your teacher to clue you in to some potentially vital information.

I remember one question-and-answer session in geography class which dealt with Great Britain's devaluation of its currency, the pound, in the 1960s. One student asked how that was important. The teacher answered and a second student came up with another, related question. It wasn't long before others got into the act and the questions kept coming. Notebooks closed, the class relaxed, and a spirited discussion ensued. Two weeks later, when the next test was given, the final question was an essay question dealing with the devaluation of the pound. Those students who had really listened picked up all twenty-five points for the essay and walked away with the top grades.

Teachers are human (yes, really!) and they can and do make mistakes. Even though your teacher may tell the class what a test will cover, take it upon yourself to decide whether there is more material which might logically be included but that he or she might have forgotten to mention. If there is, study it. No matter how frustrating it is to have items appear on a test which the teacher indicated would not be there, it does happen from time to time. If you have anticipated this sort of thing, chances are you have covered the extra material in your review and study. While others in the class are losing their minds you'll be able to answer the questions and keep moving without losing your train of thought.

Try to Outguess Your Teacher with Sample Questions and Summaries

After you have reviewed your notes, skimmed the text for bold headings and studied with flash cards or charts and whatever other study aid you may have devised, it is time to see whether you can outguess your teacher.

• Settle down with pencil and paper and begin to write down the questions *you* suspect may appear on the test. It's probably best to do this with your text closed and your notes to one side, if you can manage it. Later, check both your text and your notes to see what topics you missed and write questions to cover them as well. In constructing your questions try to keep in mind what seems important in your reading and what your teacher has made a point of stressing.

• After you have written the questions it is time to summarize the material you have studied. A summary is supposed to be brief enough to be read in just a few minutes yet substantial enough to cover the important points and ideas in a chapter, lesson or any other block of material. Try to compose your summary without having to look at your text or notes. When you have finished, glance back at the material to see what your summary left out.

Here's a hint when writing summaries for study: Write using every other line. That way, if you see you've omitted important points, it's easy to insert these items in their proper place.

• After writing sample questions and summarizing the material, put these efforts aside until the following day. During your next study session see whether you can answer the questions you prepared the day before.

• Finally, hang on to your study questions until after the test. Then take just a few minutes to see how many of the test questions you anticipated. The more you were able to spot in advance the better your test score is likely to be.

List and Define Important Words

It goes without saying that when you're faced with a vocabulary test you need to study the definitions of words. What may be a new idea for you is that this holds true for any other subject as well — English, math, science, history and so on.

What many students don't realize is how helpful it can be to make a list of important words and terms when studying for tests in these subjects. Remember Sara, the girl who did not know the meaning of "align" when it was used regarding addition and subtraction of decimal fractions? There are just as many Saras who don't know the meanings of important words in social studies, in science and even in physical education classes.

Grant was delighted when his P.E. class began the archery unit; he had always wanted to try his hand at this rustic sporting skill. Grant paid attention when the coach explained the various pieces of equipment but, to be honest, he was more interested in actually trying his luck than in learning what everything was called. Words such as "fletched" and "vane" passed over his head when the coach held up an arrow. Naturally you are ahead of the story and realize these important words appeared on the end-of-unit test. Though Grant got his share of bull's-eyes in the field, on the written test he was way off target and nearly failed.

As you read and study, make certain you know what important words mean. Keep a list of these words and write out their definitions *as they apply to the material you are studying.* Many of the words we use have multiple meanings. It is easy to attach a meaning to a word only to find that it does not make sense in a certain circumstance.

Remember Eli Whitney and his cotton gin? Years ago, an eighth-grade history student (me, who else?) knew that gin was an alcoholic drink. What gin had to do with naming Whitney's invention escaped me, nor did I ever ask because I didn't want others to laugh at me. Years later (but none too soon), I learned that "gin" was a shortened form of "engine" when used in this context. Suddenly it all came clear.

Take the time to collect important words and terms and write out their definitions as they pertain to the material you are studying. If you get stuck or find a dictionary definition that doesn't make sense, then ask your teacher for an explanation. Should you be shy or worried about others laughing at your question, catch your teacher before or after class. Remember: It is easier to ask before a test than to see one or more questions going down the tubes because you don't know the meaning of a vital word.

Overtrain for Confidence

How many times does a sprinter run the hundred-meter dash before a track meet? Once? Five times? Ten times? Fifty or a hundred or even several hundred times? No athlete who has any thought of doing well in competition would consider going to a game or meet without having practiced and trained until every move is automatic. A sprinter who suggested to his or her coach that running the hundred five or six times was enough training for the big meet could expect to hear some unpleasant comments.

But what exactly is meant by overtraining? The Olympic Games give us many examples. I have often heard a television commentator explain how a certain team became a powerhouse: The team members had been playing together for ten years, and the team practiced six to eight hours daily, six days weekly, throughout the year!

Overtraining for a test is simply a matter of studying to the point at which you know the material *completely*. Not only are you certain of the material, you have studied so thoroughly that you are absolutely positive you understand everything important that is likely to be tested. Once you have studied to this point you can be confident concerning your ability to do well on the test. Having confidence in yourself helps keep you from worrying. Worrying drains your ability and mental reserves and uses energy you need for the test.

Let's try to determine what sorts of things might be successful methods of overtraining for a test. Mark with an "x" each item you think is a logical means of overstudying to build self-confidence.

1. ___ Read every word in the text at least three times before the day of the test.
2. ___ Make certain to study at least two hours each night for four days before a test.
3. ___ Anticipate every possible question which may appear on the test and make certain you can answer each and every one.
4. ___ Review items which cause you difficulty until you are absolutely certain you understand them and have all the facts clearly in mind.
5. ___ Call your teacher on the telephone and politely ask for explanations or help when you have doubts or questions.
6. ___ Tell your parents that you won't be able to do any of your normal household chores for the duration of your studying.
7. ___ Skip some daily assignments in other classes if you have to in order to overtrain for a big test.

There is such a thing as being excessive; the ideas in items one and two are certainly that. Few students have enough time to do the reading suggested in the first item even if this sort of study were a good idea. Item two may be necessary for a major test such as a midterm or end-of-semester final, but certainly not for a smaller, chapter test of twenty general points. The point is this: Overtraining is a perfect confidence builder, but there has to be a balance between over-learning and wasting time.

Hopefully you marked items three and four. They summarize what we have been discussing for the last several pages. Item five is guaranteed to get you on your teacher's bad side. One telephone call during an entire year might be justified, especially if you have been absent. But put yourself in the teacher's place: Imagine if every student called any time he or she was struggling!

The final two ideas would get you exactly what you don't need while you're studying — a world of trouble. You may be able to beg off or postpone a really lengthy chore until after your studying is over. Just don't be foolish and get into problems with your parents over doing your chores. A long discussion or an argument with your folks only diverts everyone, especially you, from the task at hand.

As for item seven, the rest of the world does not stop when you have a test in one class. One of the worst things a student can do is to neglect daily assignments and fall behind.

Group Study Is Not Right for Everyone

Many students and teachers recommend a study group — in which a number of students from the same class gather to pool their efforts — as a great means of preparing for a test. Indeed, at their best, study groups enable students to help one another. But at their worst, study groups can prove to be a total waste of valuable time. Let's see what makes a good study group function properly.

• First, every member of the group must be ready to study. Having even one individual clowning around is distracting to everyone concerned.

• The entire group must agree when to take a break and for how long. If some members want to go through an entire session without stopping, they may be more than a little upset when others insist on taking a half hour off to prepare a snack and maybe watch a little TV.

• It is difficult enough to find a proper study location for one student. When a group meets, this difficulty is magnified. A student who is used to having the family dog around might not be bothered by the presence of someone else's dog, but to another student

Rover's friendly advances may be so distracting he or she spends more time petting the dog than contributing to the group.

• Any interruption takes time and breaks the concentration of every member of the group. Telephone calls, other students stopping to chat with one member of the group, family members coming in and out and group members catching others up on the latest news and views can all contribute to making study groups unsuccessful.

If all of these potential distractions and drawbacks are kept under control, study groups can be a real boon for many students. Classmates are given an opportunity to share their knowledge and ideas; quite often what is difficult for one student to understand is fairly easy for another student to clarify and explain. In addition, some students lack the confidence to be certain they are on the right track while working by themselves. For them a good study group — through which they experience the same gains and struggles as others — may make all the difference between doing well and fearing a test.

Before joining a study group, rate your needs on the checklist below. Remember, what is helpful to one person may be unimportant to another. If you think group study is best for you, try to work with students whose needs and goals match yours.

---

1. ____ I need to have things explained better than the text does.
2. ____ I enjoy sharing what I learn with others.
3. ____ I find it difficult to decide what questions will appear on a test.
4. ____ It is easy for me to find myself daydreaming when I study.
5. ____ I read slowly and often don't finish all the assigned reading.
6. ____ It helps me to remember if someone else is peppering me with questions.

7. ___ I can concentrate on what I am supposed to study even if my best friends are with me.
8. ___ If others make a decision about study breaks or locations that I don't agree with, it won't cause me to become upset.

There is no absolute rating scale for the above self-test. If you marked half or more of the statements, it is likely that you will profit from a study group. Students who mark only one or two items usually do their best studying on their own. In the end, the only way to see if such a method is successful for you is to take part in group study and discover for yourself whether it improves your ability to accomplish what you need to do. That, of course, is to study successfully.

Associations and Mnemonic Devices Help

It is always harder to learn and remember isolated facts than those we can associate with something we already know. Here are some examples which help explain why it is so difficult for some children to learn their basic math facts.

How many *different* math facts are shown in the following examples?

$$\begin{array}{cccc} 5 & 4 & 9 & 9 \\ +4 & +5 & -5 & -4 \end{array}$$

Do you see four entirely separate math facts above? If so, the chances are pretty good you had trouble memorizing all the basic facts in your early arithmetic classes. Perhaps you still have problems with math.

If you see two totally different sets of facts you must have had a fairly easy time learning your math combinations. This is because you see "5 + 4" and "4 + 5" as being associated or related. Naturally you then associate "9 – 5" and "9 – 4."

Those students who look at the examples and immediately associate all four had the easiest time of all in learning their basic combinations. To those who can see the relationship among all four facts in the illustration, learning elementary arithmetic facts and processes was probably a snap. Whether they knew it or not, these students were studying through association.

Associating a known fact with one you need to learn or remember is an extremely effective studying device.

For example, Chuck always struggles to remember specific dates in history. However, he can remember quite easily the *order* in which things occurred. Chuck knows that his upcoming American history test is going to ask him to match dates and events, and he's worried about how he's going to perform. He needs to remember that in 1619 the first slaves arrived in Jamestown, that in the same year a shipload of women arrived from England to become wives for the settlers, that the Pilgrims landed in 1620 and the Puritans arrived in 1630.

Here's how Chuck makes some associations to cut down on the number of dates he has to battle with: The two Jamestown events took place the same year, which was just before the Pilgrims landed. The Puritans came ten years after the Pilgrims. All Chuck has to remember is the year 1620 as the date for the Pilgrims and he can recall the other dates and events by *association*.

Association is just one form of mnemonic or memory device. Jingles or rhymes have been popular for many years in remembering dates and events. Do you remember hearing, "Columbus sailed the ocean blue in fourteen hundred ninety-two"? Rhyming "blue" and "two" helps keep the jingle in mind and is a perfect mnemonic device.

How about "I before e except after c"? This mnemonic device continues with "or when sounded as 'a' as in neighbor or weigh." There are half a dozen more lines to this particular little ditty, but I'll spare you; this one line is enough to illustrate how it helps remember what to do about the placement of "i" and "e" in words.

How many days are there in October? "Thirty days hath September, April, June and November. All the rest have thirty-one, except for February which alone hath twenty-eight." The point should be clear by now. It should also be evident that you aren't the only person who has trouble remembering important facts; that's why there are so many mnemonic devices around.

Visualization is another way to make associations. When Hank was preparing for his science test on mammals, he simply couldn't remember which camel had one hump and which had two. "That's easy," Joan told him. "The dromedary has one hump. That's because there is one hump in a capital D. The Bactrian camel has two humps, since there are two humps in a capital B."

The whole idea behind using associations and other mnemonic devices is to think of something you know and can remember and relate it to a fact or concept you need to remember. It doesn't matter how silly an association may seem so long as it helps you recall the name, date, fact or process you must know.

For years I had difficulty remembering how to spell sheriff. Was it sherrif or sheriff? Finally it struck me that the two f's in sheriff, when looked at sideways, look a lot like a pair of six-guns. From then on I've had no problem with that word. (Of course there are about ten thousand other words I have to look up, but at least I can spell sheriff correctly!)

Don't spend hours and hours trying to come up with associations; it's possible to out-think yourself and get really confused. However, it's worth a minute or two to determine whether there isn't an easy memory aid you can use. The great thing about such mnemonic devices is that once you discover one it will probably stay with you for the rest of your life.

Don't Burn Out

These days we hear lots about burnout. Police have it, teachers have it, doctors experience it and so on. In fact, even students get a case of burnout now and then.

The burnout we're interested in at the moment is the sort that happens when students study to the point where they have burned themselves out. If you want to be more exact about this, you might say that beyond a certain point studying produces diminishing returns. In still other words, an individual can begin to learn *less* the more time he or she puts in.

Overtraining builds confidence and is a powerful study aid. Burning yourself out results in fear, frustration and confusion (and probably an extremely low grade, too). The key to avoiding studying extremes — from burnout through overstudying to burnout through cramming (a word about this in a second) — is *budgeting your time*. Several sections back we talked about finding the best time to study and planning ahead for test study. Strategies such as beginning to study four days before a test help you budget enough time for the task and avoid having you burn yourself out the night before an important exam.

As long as there have been students there have been students who found themselves cramming the night before a big test. For some of us it is possible to cram just before a test and remember the facts long enough to struggle through the exam. However — and this should be no surprise to you — there are several things drastically wrong with depending on a cram session.

First, studies indicate that facts "learned" during cramming sessions are likely to fly away like a flock of pigeons the minute the test is over. Second, and perhaps just as important, is the possibility that a planned cram session won't work out. What happens if you postpone study for the history test until Thursday night and your English teacher assigns a thousand-word essay Thursday during class to be turned in Friday?

Cramming puts tremendous psychological pressure on the student. Mentally, he or she is constantly aware that within a limited time a number of facts must be learned and remembered. Just having this pressure is enough to cause many to fail at cramming successfully.

What happens when it just seems impossible to remember certain facts or processes? If we are in the midst of a last-minute cram session, our concern for the things we can't grasp is likely to cause us to lose track of things we already know. By then it has become impossible to use flash cards or devise associations to aid in recall. The solution? Plan ahead. If you must cram (and it can happen no matter how carefully you try to avoid it), just realize it is an extremely ineffective way of studying.

No discussion of burning oneself out would be complete without mentioning the all-night study session. The student relying on the all-nighter is surrounded with books, probably has the coffeepot cooking constantly, and plans to finish study in time to shower and rush to class. It's generally fairly easy to spot this student the day of the test. He or she is the one with the rings around the eyes, who falls asleep in the class preceding the one with the test and whose coffee-sodden nerves cause a frantic jump at any unexpected noise or movement. Oh, yes, he or she is also the same student who will probably stare in horror at the grade atop his or her test when it is returned.

To avoid burning yourself out, consider these suggestions:
- Plan ahead so you have several study sessions.
- Don't hit the books so long at any one session that your mind begins to phase in and out. If that happens, take a break.
- Try not to panic. Panic comes from poor planning and is an open invitation to burnout.
- Leave cramming and all-night study sessions to those who don't know better.

TEST-TAKING TIPS

- Come to class prepared to listen, take part and learn.
- Make an assignment chart — and stick to it!
- Pick the best time and place to study.
- Mnemonic devices — flash cards, information and time charts — are great study aids!
- Make sure your teacher tells you what type of test you'll be taking.
- Get into the habit of *over*training, but watch out for burnout.

CHAPTER 3

Test Day!

No matter how well you feel you have prepared yourself, the day of the test always brings just a moment or so of doubt. Have I studied enough? Did I study the right things? Have I overtrained sufficiently or am I the victim of false confidence? These and other questions will be answered soon enough.

Be Prepared

"Be prepared" is not just a motto for Boy Scouts. It is a concept for everyone who seriously hopes to do well on tests. If you have followed the suggestions in the previous section of this book, the chances are you are prepared. Of course, just how well prepared you actually are won't be determined until you take the test, but if you have done what we suggested, you should be pleased with your score.

Preparation involves effort, as you well know. Moreover, it requires *honest effort* on your part. All the flash cards and information charts in the world won't help if you simply look at them and make no effort to remember the information contained on them. You can have the best study location in the world, with proper lighting, a great desk and no interruptions, but it does you no good if you don't use your time to concentrate on the task at hand. Carefully taken notes don't do much good if the note taker only glances at them instead of reviewing them with the idea of really learning the material. As you can see, it is all too easy to fool yourself into thinking you have prepared when, in reality, you only went through the motions. Should this be the case, you'll discover your error on test day.

What happens if you have tried in all good faith to prepare and then flubbed your first test? It's not the end of the world. Don't let panic and frustration take over. Instead, go back and review your study efforts and try to determine what went wrong. Some things look easy and turn out to be difficult and require considerable time to master. Many people view a ten- or twelve-speed bicycle as a breeze to ride because "all those gears take the work out of riding." Nothing could be further from the truth. In order to reach the point at which a person can ride a bicycle one hundred miles uphill and down in a single day, weeks and months of training, practice and conditioning are required. Mastering the basics of taking tests successfully is not unlike this. It takes practice, and practice requires effort.

Hopefully, your first test will go well and you will be immediately aware that the suggestions we've been talking about really work. If your first test or even tests *don't* go all that well, hang in and don't give up. Analyze your study efforts to see where things went wrong and correct those errors the next time. Once you master the steps in preparing for tests you are well on your way to mastering the tests themselves.

Be Early

Last-minute hurrying and rushing around can be so mind-bending that much of your careful preparation goes down the drain under the stress of being late. Plan ahead so you have enough time to get to the test location with a few minutes to spare. If the test is scheduled for the first thing in the morning, make a point of leaving for school a fèw minutes early. For tests given later in the day, don't stop to check the latest gossip on the way to class if that means you'll just beat the bell. Carry with you everything necessary for the test so you can avoid having to race from one end of the building to the other in order to grab something from your locker. The knowledge that you are late or likely to be tardy creates panic — the one thing no one needs on test day.

Don't Skip Meals

Although it's important to get to class on time, don't skip breakfast. That nourishment will help get your brain in gear. You'll also be able to concentrate better during the test if your stomach isn't growling. If your test falls in the afternoon, be sure to eat well at lunch. If you plan to use lunchtime for last-minute reviewing, at least bring along a piece of fruit.

Arrive with the Proper Materials

When was the last time someone in your class had to ask the teacher for a pen or pencil or sheet of paper in order to tackle a test? Probably not all that long ago. Knowing what materials you will need for a test is usually a matter of listening to what the teacher says a day or two prior to the test. If your teacher has a hang-up about pens and tells you to write in pencil, then do just that. Should your teacher mention the need for wide-lined paper, it is poor planning to arrive with college-ruled sheets in your notebook. Sometimes machine-scored tests require a number-two pencil. If that's the case, be sure you come properly equipped. Pencils break or become dull and must be sharpened. Bring two or even three sharpened pencils to class and avoid wasting valuable time at the pencil sharpener when you could be answering another question or two.

Any frantic last-minute search for necessary materials causes confusion. Confusion breeds frustration, and fear or panic can follow more quickly than seems possible. Remember Robert, who found such success with the flash cards he constructed? For some reason Robert failed to hear his teacher tell the class that a certain science test would be open-book. Robert arrived in class well prepared but without his text (and since the test was open-book the questions were that much more difficult). Don't find yourself in a similar situation, or even worse, because you reach class without the proper materials.

Listen to and Read the Test Directions

Even though most tests have written directions at the beginning, you can expect nearly every teacher to add to them with oral instructions. Listen to these oral instructions. *Really listen!* Don't just let the words flow over you while you check out Leonard's new haircut or Mary's letter jacket. All the preparation in the world can get shot out of the saddle when you fail to listen to, and then follow, oral instructions. Here's one such instruction some students found painful:

> "This is a four-page test. I'm going to separate the pages for grading. Be sure to write your name in the upper right-hand corner of each page. Only pages with names on them will be graded."

Is it necessary to say more about this example? That particular teacher gave tests which were formatted so that she always graded every first page, then all the second pages, and so on. The strange thing was that even after the first such test, which was a disaster for the half dozen students who did not listen to instructions, there always seemed to be at least one member of the class who did not listen on future tests. Don't dig a hole for yourself by failing to listen to and heed oral instructions. That's the time your teacher will mention special questions, any errors he or she has caught in the printing, time limits, extra credit or bonus points and the like. If your teacher says something you don't understand or could not hear, ask for an explanation. Don't be shy about requesting more information.

Once the oral instructions are over, it's time for you to put your name on the test paper. Do this even before reading the written directions. It seems strange, but once a test has begun one of the easiest things in the world to forget is the need to write your name on the test.

Next you need to read the test directions and make certain you understand what you are supposed to do. Exercise a bit of caution when doing this. Some years ago, the Singer Company put out a new motion picture projector and placed on each projector a sticker which said, "Before doing it your way try it our way." In other words, there is a definite, precise, correct way to do certain things. If there is any doubt in your mind, spend another few seconds rereading the instructions. Should you still be unsure, ask your teacher for whatever clarification you need. Never fall into the trap of assuming you know how to take a test without reading the instructions. Nancy fell victim when she plunged into a multiple-choice test without discovering she was supposed to mark the *incorrect* choice in each set of answers. Midway through the test Nancy realized there were several correct answers and called that fact to her teacher's attention. The teacher mentioned the directions, class members gave Nancy a big cheer, and Nancy found herself out of time long before she was able to redo the first half of the test and then finish the rest of the questions.

Once you are certain you understand the directions, it's just you and the test. Go for it!

TEST-TAKING TIPS

- Get to class on time — *with* the materials you need for the test!
- Make sure you've nourished your brain by eating a good breakfast or lunch.
- *Really listen to* and *really read* the test directions.

CHAPTER 4

Meeting the Test Face to Face

Up to now we've been concerned with why students do poorly on tests and how to prepare for tests. Now it's time to look at the various types of tests you can expect to meet, and learn how best to master each of them.

You will be taking some sample tests in this section. These will illustrate the various forms of tests and offer you an opportunity to check your own recall of material we have covered thus far.

Objective vs. Essay Tests

You are more likely to encounter objective tests than essay tests. Objective tests have a definite answer which is acceptable. This answer may be the best choice in a multiple-choice test. It may be either true or false or even yes or no. In some objective tests the student is required to match an item, name or date in one column with a related answer in a second column. There is also the completion or short-answer objective test (sometimes called fill-in tests). Usually there is only one possible answer, though from time to time completion tests may have a couple of acceptable answers.

The great thing about objective tests is that they don't require a lot of writing on your part. At most it takes only a few words to finish a completion question. Multiple-choice and matching tests usually require a letter for an answer, and writing either true or false takes about two seconds. A well-written objective test is a real test of whether or not the student understands the material. Teachers give them for this reason and because they are easy for students to understand and easy for the teachers to grade.

Essay tests, in contrast, require lots of writing, sometimes many pages for just one question. This allows students to tell everything they know about a subject (it also means students get writer's cramp from all that pencil pushing). From the teacher's point of view, an essay test is difficult to grade. A stack of essay tests can mean good-bye weekend because of the time required to mark each test. (Throw in the fact some students have handwritings that make a doctor's prescription look great, and it's small wonder so many teachers wear glasses.) It's also something of a *subjective* appraisal of whether or not a student has answered a question sufficiently.

Let's look at these various test types and see what you need to know about each in order to get the upper hand.

Multiple-Choice Tests

Multiple-choice tests present a number of possible answers, only one of which is correct. You may be asked to indicate the correct answer by underlining it, by circling it or by writing the letter before the answer in a space. The questions may be actual questions with three to five possible answers to choose from, or they may be written as a statement which is completed correctly by one of the possible choices. To complicate things still further, you may run into multiple-choice tests which may have no correct answer choices or have all answer choices correct. Some fun, huh? Before we try our hand at a few practice multiple-choice questions, here are a few tips which help deal with this form of objective test:

• If it is written as a question, try to think of the correct answer before you read the choices.

• Be sure to read all the choices. Sometimes one choice is better than another which may look good to you.

• If you don't know the correct answer, cross out any answers you know are *incorrect*. This narrows the field.

• Pick the answer from those remaining which seems most reasonable. (Sometimes you luck out and have only one remaining answer. Even though you did not realize it was correct, through a process of elimination you have determined that all the others are wrong.)

Let's take a look at some multiple-choice questions. These will be written in several different ways to give you a look at the various forms such questions may take.

Directions: Choose the one best answer to each question. Write that answer's letter in the space provided.

1. ___ Winnie-the-Pooh was a stuffed
        a. tiger
        b. cow
        c. bear
        d. dog

2. ___ Who wrote the Winnie-the-Pooh stories?
        a. Robert Louis Stevenson
        b. A. A. Milne
        c. Joel Chandler Harris
        d. Michael Bond

3. ___ Winnie-the-Pooh's human friend was
        a. Charles
        b. Carl
        c. Christopher
        d. Carol
        e. Robin

4. ___ Among Winnie-the Pooh's animal friends we met
      a. Piglet
      b. Owl
      c. Kanga
      d. Eeyore
      e. all of the above

The four questions you just answered are four common ways multiple choice questions appear. (The correct answers were 1-c, 2-b, 3-c and 4-e.)

At times, teachers get a little tricky when they write multiple-choice questions. Here's one such example.

---

5. ___ Which animal did Winnie-the-Pooh not have as a friend?
      a. Owl
      b. Piglet
      c. Heffalump
      d. Baby Roo
      e. all of the above

Unless you read the word "not" in the question the likely choice is "e". Of course, the answer is "c". *Watch out for negative questions which contain "not," "no," "never" and similar words.*

Another type of multiple-choice question which can be really rough is illustrated next.

---

6. ___ When Winnie-the-Pooh tried to raid the honey tree, which of the following were involved?
      a. Christopher Robin
      b. a balloon
      c. an umbrella
      d. none of the above
      e. all of the above

If you can find one correct answer, you know "d" can't be right. If you can locate two or three correct answers, then "e" has to be correct, which it is. Note: Don't get too clever and assume that "e" also would include "d" since "d" is above "e." Both "d" and "e" refer to answers "a", "b" and "c".

Here's a final form of multiple-choice question which really requires that you know your material. Not many teachers use it, but you should at least know about this kind of question.

---

7. ___ Which of the following events involved Winnie-the-Pooh and his friends? (Choose from among e, f, g and h.)

    a. Eeyore loses his tail
    b. Pooh and Eeyore nearly catch a Woozle
    c. Piglet meets a Heffalump
    d. Kanga and Baby Roo come to the forest
    e. a, b, c
    f. a, c, d
    g. a, b, c, d
    h. b, c, d

The answer is "f." If you encounter this type of question, first find an answer you are sure of. Then cross out any of the choices which don't include that answer. If you can find an answer you know is wrong, cross out any choices which include that answer. Then repeat the process with another correct answer or incorrect answer. Hopefully, you'll reach the point at which only one choice is left.

Now that you know how to deal with multiple-choice questions and the forms they take, take this little self-test.

Directions: Write the letter of the best answer in the space provided.

1. ___ What makes it difficult to do well on tests?
   a. not reading the assignment
   b. failure to listen
   c. excessive absences
   d. forgetting
   e. all of these
2. ___ Preparing for a test requires
   a. bringing materials to class
   b. having an ideal study situation
   c. studying right after school
   d. joining a study group
3. ___ The best time to study
   a. is before watching TV
   b. is after watching TV
   c. is with a friend
   d. varies
4. ___ Note taking ___ recall.
   a. helps
   b. guarantees
   c. restricts
   d. inhibits
5. ___ Mnemonic devices could include
   a. associations
   b. flash cards
   c. visual pictures
   d. none of these
   e. all of these

Check your answers on page 83. Doubtless you scored a perfect test. If so, congratulations. If not, look back at the second and third chapters and see why you missed what you did.

Matching Tests

It doesn't hurt to think of matching tests as huge multiple-choice tests. Usually a matching test confronts you with two columns of related items. Your task, of course, is to match each item in one column with the related answer in the second column. When you look at the first item in the first column you have to consider every answer in the other column as a possible answer. Talk about multiple choice! However, after you use an answer in the second column you don't have to think about it anymore, so your number of choices gets smaller as you make matches (unless your teacher is tricky and allows you to use answers more than once, but we'll discuss that in a moment or two).

Here are some tips which make matching tests a little less impossible:

• Begin with the easiest item in the list, one you know for sure, and match it.

• Cross out each answer in the answer column as you use it (but don't black it out; a single line will do the job, just in case you need to be able to read that answer again).

• If one column is longer than the other because some answers are included which won't be used, always work from the shorter, or question column. Otherwise you'll probably find yourself looking for a match that does not exist.

• When you have matched all the answers you can and still have not finished, make the best guesses you can with the remaining choices. Don't leave unmatched answers: they are obviously incorrect. An educated guess at least gives you a chance.

Let's take a look at several forms of matching tests.

Directions: Match the answer at the right with the item it best matches at the left. Write the letter before the answer in the space provided.

1. ___	Moby Dick	a. shark
2. ___	Bambi	b. whale
3. ___	Jaws	c. horse
4. ___	Flicka	d. deer
5. ___	Paddington	e. bear

Don't you wish all your matching tests were this easy! The correct answers are: 1-b, 2-d, 3-a, 4-c, 5-e.

Many teachers include extra choices in the answer column. These are called *foils* and are intended to make it more difficult to guess correctly if you don't really know your material. A test of this type looks something like this:

Directions: Write the letter before each character in the right-hand column in the space before the author who created it at the left. You won't use some of the answers in the column at the right.

1. ___ Peter Benchley		a. Paddington
2. ___ Felix Salten		b. Moby Dick
3. ___ Herman Melville		c. Flicka
4. ___ Michael Bond		d. Winnie-the-Pooh
5. ___ Mary O'Hara		e. Bambi
6. ___ Walter Farley		f. Silver Chief
		g. Jaws
		h. Black Stallion

Teachers who use this sort of matching test make things a bit more difficult. However, approach any matching test in the same way. Match those you know to cut down on the choices, then take your best shot at the rest. (The answers, just in case you are in doubt, are: 1-g, 2-e, 3-b, 4-a, 5-c and 6-h.)

Sometimes it is possible for one question to help answer another. When this occurs, by all means take advantage of the help offered. In this case you might have recalled that A.A. Milne wrote about Winnie-the-Pooh because that was an example in the multiple-choice tests. If you made that association, it immediately ruled out one of the foils.

A third form of matching test you may encounter allows you to use answers more than once. Just to add to your delight we'll set these answers up in a list rather than a column.

Directions: Write the letter of each animal in the first list below in front of the name or item it best matches in the numbered list which follows. Some answers will be used more than once.

---

a. Bambi
b. Flicka
c. Lassie
d. Paddington
e. Winnie-the-Pooh

1. ___ Flower
2. ___ Wyoming
3. ___ Scotland
4. ___ Eeyore
5. ___ Thumper
6. ___ London
7. ___ Thunderhead

Since you can't rule out any of the answers, this sort of matching test may be the most difficult. Nothing beats being completely prepared and knowing the answers. Otherwise, when in doubt, make a good guess. (The correct answers here are: 1-a, 2-b, 3-c, 4-e, 5-a, 6-d and 7-b.)

Let's take another self-test to determine how much of what you've been reading is being retained.

Directions: In the matching test on the following page, match the description at the right with the item at the left by writing the letter in the space provided. You won't use every description.

1. ___ mnemonic device	a. short overview of material
2. ___ summary	b. studying more than needed
3. ___ define	c. sample questions
4. ___ overlearn	d. relating one thing to another
5. ___ association	e. memory aid
	f. confidence
	g. give the meaning

You can check your answers on page 83. In the above test, two answers might be possible for mnemonic device. If you chose one of them, you later had to change it because it was required for another matching. This is why you cross out used answers but don't black them out entirely.

True/False Tests

You will probably take as many true/false tests as any other single type of test. That's fine with me, you say; what could be easier than deciding whether a statement is correct or incorrect? And it's true, this kind of objective test is one you can really get the upper hand of, provided you have prepared adequately. Otherwise, a true/false test can just about drive you over the edge.

What follows are some tips to keep in mind when confronted with true/false tests. Remember, though, that your teachers know these ideas, too, and may get tricky and set up some questions which are just the opposite of what you might expect. As you well know by now, there is absolutely no substitute for knowing the material.

• A statement is false if any part of it is incorrect. This holds true even if twenty words are true and only one is false.

• Statements which include such words as always, never, constantly, all, none, etc. are likely to be false. (Here's where a teacher can trip you up by writing a true question using these words.)

• In general (not always), extremely long statements are likely to be false.

• Watch out for statements in which "not" is used to make things just the opposite of what they seem.

With these good thoughts to guide you, let's see how you do with this sample true/false test.

Directions: Write "true" or "false" in the space provided to indicate whether a statement is correct or incorrect.

---

1. ___ The creature in *Jaws* was a great white hammerhead shark.
2. ___ The people of Amityville depended on tourists for much of their income.
3. ___ One thing which made the presence of the shark so bad was that the townspeople were trying to have the beaches open for Labor Day vacationers.
4. ___ Chief Brody conquered the shark through his knowl edge of the sea.
5. ___ Though Quint knew a lot about sharks, this one managed to kill him.

In this short test, the first four answers are false and the last is true. In the first and third statements, a single word makes the difference. "Jaws" was not a *hammerhead* shark, and the townspeople were worried because the presence of the shark occurred around *Memorial* Day, at the beginning of the summer tourist season, not Labor Day, the end. In the second statement, half a word (ville) makes it false; the name of the town was *Amity* (Amityville was the locale of a different kind of horror movie). The fourth question is out and out incorrect; Brody was deathly afraid of the sea.

Once in a while a teacher will throw you a curve and present you with a yes/no test. This sort of test is handled exactly the same as a true/false test. The difference is that you are answering questions either "yes" or "no" instead of deciding whether statements are true or false.

When you finish the self-test which follows, check your answers on page 83.

Directions: Mark each statement "true" or "false" in the space provided.

---

1. ____ It is necessary to begin studying for every test at least four days in advance.
2. ____ Flash cards are always the best study device for math.
3. ____ Writing and answering sample questions is a better study method than reviewing notes.
4. ____ Study groups provide the best way for all poor readers to learn difficult material.
5. ____ Cramming is a good way to prevent burnout.

Completion and Short-Answer Tests

A completion test requires that you supply a missing word or phrase which finishes the statement correctly. A short-answer test asks you to answer a question with one or a few words. A fill-in test is just another name for a completion test.

The really nasty thing about a completion test is that you have to know the answer in order to provide it. There are no choices from which to select, and you can't just decide whether it is true or false.

Here are a few tips which may help you master this kind of test:

- Sometimes teachers give you a hint by making the sentence singular or plural. (If the question says something about "... are _____" you know the answer can't be Patrick Henry because subject and verb would not agree.)
- The length of the blank may help tell you whether an exceptionally long or really short word or phrase is needed. (Teachers may trip you up here by making all blanks the same length or leaving lots of space for a short answer.)
- If you have even a remote idea as to the correct answer, give it your best guess. A space left blank is obviously not going to score you a point.

Try your hand at this completion test.

Directions: Supply the missing word which correctly completes each statement.

---

1. James _____ was known as 007.
2. The number 007 meant a secret agent was licensed to _____.
3. Agent 007's immediate superior was known as _____.
4. Ms. Moneypenny was the _____ who was extremely fond of 007.
5. James was employed by the _____ government.

Since you've probably seen some of the James Bond movies, you knew the answer to the first question. As for questions two and three, Bond was licensed to *kill,* and his superior was called *M.* Question four is an example of taking an educated guess. If you didn't remember that Moneypenny was a secretary, you knew she was female since she was "Ms." The answer "woman" might not be what was called for but is actually correct and might earn you some credit. The last question is a kind you will encounter from time to time. "British" is the correct answer but you could argue "English" since Bond works out of London.

Again, a not completely correct answer may get you some credit. (Good preparation gives you a shot at coming up with a reasonable answer when you don't know the one the teacher is hoping for.)

Let's see how a short-answer test is different from the completion or fill-in test you just took. As you take this test, and when you take *any* short-answer test, remember this one tip: If you don't know the answer, always write down something you do know which seems close; you may get full credit if you are close enough to what the teacher expected, and you may get partial credit if you are fairly close. What have you got to lose?

Directions: Write the correct answer in each blank.

1. Samuel Clemens wrote under the pen name
   _____.

2. Clemens's pen name came from the time he spent on the Mississippi River as a _____.

3. Tom Sawyer was the boy who gave his cat a dose of pain-killer in the book _____.

4. Another of Tom's adventures involved whitewashing a _____.

5. Tom's aunt was a wonderful woman because she _____.

The answers: Samuel Clemens was better known as *Mark Twain*. He got the name from the time he spent as a *riverboat pilot*. (A depth of two, or *twain* fathoms meant the boat could navigate safely through a river. It was the crew's duty to shout, "Mark One, Mark Twain.") Tom was featured in *The Adventures of Tom Sawyer*. Perhaps his best-remembered adventure was the scene in which he convinced others to help him whitewash a *picket fence*. Tom's aunt *loved him and always forgave him for what he did*. (Did you say she loved him? Or that she forgave him? Each was worth half credit. Or did you have another choice worth partial credit? The main thing is not to have left the question blank.)

Now let's make a quick check of your test mastery thus far.

Directions: Write the missing word or term in each blank.

---

1. Multiple-choice, true/false and completion tests are examples of _____ tests.
2. Tests set up in two columns are usually _____ tests.
3. If any part of a statement is incorrect, the statement _____ is false.
4. Extra answers in a test are known as _____.
5. Another name for a completion test is a _____ test.

Turn to page 83 to see how well you scored.

General Test-Taking Tactics

Before we talk about essay tests, let's spend a few minutes looking at some general tactics which can improve your chances of mastering tests.

• Though we've mentioned it before, be absolutely certain you understand the directions and know exactly what is expected of you.

• The same thing applies when it comes to reading each and every question carefully. It is terribly easy to have something in mind which causes you to misread a question. (Remember my problems with carbon dioxide?)

• It is always a good idea to spend a few seconds skimming over any test before you actually begin writing answers.

— Determine whether the entire test is made up of the same type of questions.

— Check the test for length.

— Try to estimate how long it will take you to

complete the entire test and how much time you can spend on individual sections or each page.

— Then take a quick look at the clock and set some mental time limits by pages or sections.

• It is always a good idea to do what you know best first. If one part of the test is easier, do that part first. If some questions are simple, mark them before you tackle the brain-busters. Not only does this strategy guarantee you some quick points, it also helps relieve any tension you have concerning the test. Knowing you have done part of a test goes a long way toward relaxing you so you can deal with the harder parts.

• Keep watching for one question which contains the answer to another. Teachers often present a question and then, a few questions later, ask another which answers the first question. (Remember A.A. Milne and Winnie-the-Pooh when we dealt with multiple-choice tests?)

• When you don't know an answer, take an educated guess. *Don't guess if there is a penalty for guessing* (such as the loss of two points for a wrong answer). The better prepared you are, the more educated your guesses become.

• Keep an eye open for important or key words which will either give you a clue to the correct response or trigger your memory.

• If you get stuck, don't spend too much time on a difficult question. Go on with the test and, if you have time, come back to the question which had you stumped. By then you may have discovered the answer within the test, or something else may have helped you remember the necessary answer (sometimes you simply don't remember the first time you look at a question). Just don't forget you have left an unanswered question and turn your test in before returning to the stumper.

• Avoid making a simple question difficult by looking for a trick. Most questions mean exactly what they appear to. Teachers realize tests are hard enough without deliberately making them deceptive.

• Don't change an answer unless you have a good reason for doing so. Studies have proven that your first impression is more likely to be correct than a later one. This is not to say you should never change an answer. It does indicate, however, that there are limited instances in which you should do so. If you discover information in a later question which proves one of your answers is wrong, then obviously you have a reason for changing it.

• Keep track of the time as you work and remember the goals you set in regard to each page or section of the test.

Pop (or Surprise) Quizzes and Tests

There is no surefire way to prepare for pop quizzes and surprise tests except to make absolutely certain you keep up with your assignments. The study tips and suggestions we have covered all apply to preparing for the time you enter the classroom, pop quiz or no pop quiz.

If you know you have read your assignments, and are certain you have followed a study plan which works for you, then you are halfway home when it comes to dealing with the unannounced quiz or test.

One of the things about pop quizzes which helps defeat some students is the tension which comes as a result of the unexpected test. Most of this tension is because of the uncertainty of one's ability to pass a test for which he or she has not prepared. Students who spend most of their energy coping with the reality of the surprise test have little left to spend on passing the test. But since *you* have your assignments up to date you won't be in the position of having to overcome your fear of being unprepared.

Even so, everyone could probably use a few pointers.

• Not all surprise tests should be total surprises. Many teachers clue you in the day before by saying such things as "Make certain you read this assignment so we can cover it in class tomorrow," or "Be sure you are up to date on your assignments." These and similar statements don't *guarantee* a pop quiz the following day, but for certain teachers they do become a positive indication that something special is on the horizon.

• Watch for scoring patterns on short objective pop tests. Teachers are pressed for time and some try to make things easier for themselves by setting up tests with scoring patterns to make grading quicker. If you can detect such a pattern, it enables you to check your own test and often gives you a chance to decide on a correct answer when you are in doubt. For example, a ten-question true/false test with an answer pattern of T, T, F, F, T, T, F, F, T, T is easy to score. So is a multiple-choice test whose answers form a pattern such as a, b, c, d, a, b, c, d. (Don't count on passing tests by discovering scoring patterns — most tests don't have such deliberate patterns, nor are most teachers that predictable. However, if you find that a teacher uses these patterns on pop quizzes, you would be foolish not to take advantage of your discovery.)

Essay Questions

An essay test allows you to "let go" and include every bit of information you have learned about a certain topic. This may be a bonus or a disaster, depending upon how well you know your material and how capable you are when it comes to expressing your thoughts and ideas.

Essay-test answers come in long and short varieties. You may find yourself answering half a dozen questions in short essays or one long hummer whose answer requires several pages. It is always a good idea, on a separate sheet of paper, to list the ideas or facts you wish to include in your answer. This holds true no matter how long the essay answer will be. As you write your actual answer, check off each fact or concept as it becomes part of your essay. Then check your list to make certain you didn't forget to make use of something important once you got involved with your answer. For the question, "Explain why the people of England did not retain Winston Churchill as prime minister following World War II," your listing of facts may be as simple as this:

- People wanted to forget war.
- The English related Churchill and his party to the war.
- The liberals running against him promised prosperity after the privations of past years.
- Some would have voted liberal in earlier years but realized that Churchill's party offered the nation its best chance at victory.
- Voters often demand change following major events.
- Many viewed the war as the result of failed conservative policies.

Some students find it helps to put their ideas into outline form. Such an outline should be extremely simple, otherwise you'll spend all your time constructing the outline and have too little time for your essay. An outline for the above question might be as simple as this:

I. Conservatives got blamed for allowing war
II. Churchill associated in minds of many with war
III. Change after war normal
IV. Liberals promised prosperity

As you write your essay, make sure to include the information you noted in proper order as you follow your outline. It's as basic as that.

There are a number of key words teachers use to tell you what sort of essay answer they expect. We won't try to list all of these words, but discussing a few will give you a leg up on understanding this type of test.

• *Compare* has been a favorite essay instruction as long as there have been essay tests. When you are asked to compare life in China today with life during the Cultural Revolution, your teacher is asking you to tell how things are now and how the same sort of things were then. In a question of this type discuss how things are the same and how they differ.

• When you are asked to *contrast* two items — such as junior high and elementary school — you are supposed to tell how the two experiences are different.

• Lots of times you may be asked to compare *and* contrast something; in this case tell how the items are alike and how they are different.

• If you are told to *define* a term or idea you are to tell what it means.

• When you *describe* something, such as London during the Blitz, you need to state facts which tell how it looked and what was happening. Use facts, not your opinions, in your description.

• Many teachers ask you to *discuss* a topic. When you discuss those things that led to the Civil War, you will tell about all the things which helped start the war and how each was significant. In a discussion question, always include reasons something was good or bad or important or how it influenced events.

• When asked to *explain,* you are supposed to tell how and why something occurred or was important, etc. For example, explaining how the cotton gin helped start the Civil War would require you to know that the invention allowed quick removal of cotton seeds and how this resulted in a demand for more land and more slaves.

• To *illustrate* something, you may draw a picture or graph or you may tell about it in words.

• *Justify* is an instruction which means you have to give reasons something is good or bad. Remember, these are reasons or facts, not just your opinions.

• A favorite direction of some teachers includes the word *prove*. This instruction indicates that you have to present facts and ideas which show without doubt why something is good or bad, why it happened or perhaps how two things are alike or related.

• When you are asked to *review* a topic, you need to include the main points and explain why they are important.

• Another very common essay test asks you to *summarize* a topic. This simply indicates that you need to shorten a rather lengthy happening or description so that you cover all the important facts briefly.

Though there are many other instructions you will encounter while taking essay tests, those we just covered give you a good idea of what to expect when your teacher announces an upcoming essay test.

Write every essay-test answer as though you were writing an essay in English, even if you're taking a social-studies test. Use sentences, and put your sentences into paragraphs of related ideas. Try to spell every word correctly, and use proper grammar. No matter how hurried you are, use your best penmanship. When a teacher has to struggle with your writing, no matter how great he or she is, there is always the possibility you will lose credit just because it becomes too difficult to figure out what you were trying to say.

As with objective tests, you'll need to keep an eye on the clock. It is easy during a long essay question to get caught up in your answer and run out of time before you include all the points you should. So long as you have time, write everything you know unless your teacher has already instructed you to limit each answer to a certain number of lines or pages.

One word of advice regarding essay tests: Write *something* no matter how uncertain you are of the answer. If you know anything remotely concerning the question, put your pencil to the paper and write the facts you know. Even if you miss the main idea of the question, you may get partial credit for some of the material you do know.

Another helpful hint: If you know your test will be in the form of an essay, it is sometimes useful to write a few sample essays at home the night before — after you've studied the material. Close all books and time yourself. Go back and refer to your notes to see what details you left out or might have included. Often you'll be under less pressure on test day because you've already practiced.

Standardized Tests Are the Same, Only Different

There is nothing about a standardized test which should give you any problems as far as understanding the test is concerned. This isn't to say that some of the questions aren't real brain-busters. It's just that the test itself is made up of various forms of objective questions.

Schools use standardized tests to see how their students compare with other schools in the state or across the nation. The great thing about standardized tests is they are not used to determine your grade. However, they may be used to decide which classes you will take or will be allowed to take, which is a good reason you want to do as well on them as possible.

Juniors and seniors in high school take special standardized tests such as the ACT (American College Testing) or SAT (Scholastic Aptitude Test) to become eligible for entry into certain colleges.

The standardized tests you are likely to take may include the California Achievement Test or the Iowa Test of Basic Skills. Both deal with facts and content you have learned or are supposed to have learned.

Aptitude tests are special tests which help indicate what sort of abilities you have in a number of areas and are used as one means of helping you know what sort of career may be best for you.

Standardized tests are scored by machine, which means that they are usually answered by marking the circle or rectangle beside the correct answer. This almost always means that the test is some form of multiple-choice or true/false test.

You can't very well study for a standardized test. Such tests are designed to cover a year's work or several years' study. However, every time you crack a book you are, in some way, preparing for a standardized test you will take one day.

Standardized tests are almost always *timed,* that is, you will be told how many minutes you have for the test or for specific sections of the test. Once you know how much time is available, glance over the test and set some goals. Then remember to check the time occasionally and compare your location in the test with the goals you have set.

Everything you already know about taking objective tests applies to standardized tests, so there is no need to go over tactics such as not bogging down on difficult questions and the like. Here's one tip to remember, however:

Many standardized tests include an answer choice such as "don't know." It may be true that you do not know the answer, but "don't know" is never a correct answer. You won't get any points for marking this choice. In addition, don't confuse "don't know" with "not given." Some standardized tests use "not given" as a choice which may be the correct response. In such cases answers which look almost correct are always included in an effort to make certain you know what you are talking about.

One tip to remember: Keep your test and answer sheet close together. You'd be amazed at how much wasted time is spent reaching to the other side of a desk, locating the line on which you are to mark the answer and then referring back to the question again.

Some students choke and become tense and nervous over standardized tests. And certainly they can be imposing — some of them have forty or fifty pages. But don't let them get you down. Even if you blow one part of such a test, it isn't the end of the world. Put a poor session behind you and think of the next one as a brand-new opportunity. There's no reason to let one upset throw you off stride.

TEST-TAKING TIPS

- Analyze multiple-choice, matching and completion test questions before jumping to conclusions.
- Watch for trick words — such as "never," "always" and "not" — when taking an objective test.
- Outline your essay question answer before actually beginning to write.
- Watch for key words in essay questions that tell you what to do.
- Keep an eye on the clock — and answer the questions you know first.

CHAPTER 5

Tips for Taking Tests in Various Subjects

W hat you have already learned applies to tests in any and all subjects. There are, in addition, a few tips or ideas which may help you master tests in certain specific subject areas.

Math

Let's begin with math, since this subject bothers a great many students. These tips on test preparation and test taking should help.

• Don't fall into the trap of assuming you can solve a certain type of problem. Try to solve every practice problem you find in the text pages that are to be covered on a test.

• Since each step in math builds on previous steps, be sure you understand these processes before test day.

• On test day, take with you every aid your teacher will allow. If you are permitted to have a list of formulas, problem samples and calculators, be sure to have them. There's no reason to make things harder than they have to be.

• Don't linger on a difficult problem. Come back to it when you have completed the easier ones.

• Try to estimate answers before actually working out problems. This helps you spot answers which are totally out of the ballpark.
• Be sure to show your work and label answers, if that is what the directions call for.

Science

Even though you study a variety of topics in science, a few ideas about taking science tests will apply to most situations.
• A good way to prepare for science tests is to study carefully the diagrams and illustrations found in your text. Almost always some questions will be taken from these pictures and drawings.
• Much of science involves vocabulary. Keep a list of important words to review just before the test.
• Watch for information in one part of the test which answers a question in another part. This seems to happen more often in science tests.
• Try to retain mental pictures of diagrams and processes from the text so you can relate them to illustrations you see on the test. Or better yet, trace the diagram, shut your book and then label all the relevant parts.

Social Studies

Most of your social studies tests will involve history, geography and basic economics.
• Set up a time chart and study the order in which important events occur.
• If you will be asked to do map work on your test, spend some time with a blank outline map learning important locations.
• Try to think of relationships when you study and during test time. Remember who is related to what event and how one event helped cause another.

• If your teacher is known for his or her essay tests, always come prepared with some key ideas and main topics to include in your essay answers. You can also practice writing out a few of these at home.

English

English tests often cover grammar, writing skills or literature.

• Review special grammar rules just before a usage test. If you can associate rules with mnemonic devices it usually helps. (I used to remember the difference between "may" and "can" by recalling a drawing of a little guy asking to carry a large woman across a puddle. "You may if you can," she told him.)

• Try to think of grammar rules in groups, such as which pronouns are used together, where adverbs and adjectives are placed in a sentence, etc.

• Don't become so involved with a special writing skill — such as the use of irony or metaphor — that you forget basic skills such as sentence structure, paragraphing and proper punctuation and capitalization.

• Literature tests will ask for more than a simple recitation of what happened in the story. During your reading and when you're studying, watch for and remember how characters changed, what caused these changes, what events affected the characters and how the setting was important to the characters and the overall story.

Foreign Languages

Though foreign languages seem totally different than what you are used to, foreign language tests don't have to stump you.

• Watch for words which are similar to English words in spelling and meaning. Such words are called "cognates" and are derived from a common base, so they share the same meaning and similar spelling.

• Review related groups of words together and try to associate them with one another. It's easier to remember food names, for example, when you think of them as a menu.

• Be certain you understand the rules of pronunciation perfectly. If you mispronounce a word, you are more likely to spell it incorrectly.

• Try to form a mental picture of difficult words, phrases and idioms. Mnemonic devices are a big help here.

• Remember, all foreign languages make sense. Look for and then remember patterns and logical constructions.

Spelling

In elementary school, spelling is usually a separate subject, but in the higher grades, spelling tests may come as part of any class.

• Make a list of the words you are expected to spell. If your teacher says something such as, "Learn to spell the important terms and words," then make your own list. Don't try to study words which are scattered throughout the text.

• Use any mnemonic device possible to help spell difficult words. Finding small words in large ones is good, as is relating a new word to another word you can already spell.

• Learn the basic rules for spelling, such as how adding prefixes and suffixes makes changes in the root word.

• Make use of aids such as "i before e," but remember that there are exceptions to these rules.
• Remember that the way words are used in the sciences and in social studies may be different from what you know or expect. Also, many specialized words have letter patterns within them that you may not be used to. For example, languages other than English contain words with letters other than "u" following "q," such as Qatar (the Arabian country) and the Qatarra Depression in the Egyptian desert.

Vocabulary

Every class has its own special vocabulary which you need to know not only for vocabulary tests but to understand the class content.
• If the test offers you definitions from which to choose, always try to come up with a meaning before you look at the choices.
• If the test calls for you to supply the definition, don't waste time if you get stuck. Come back after doing the rest of the list. Sometimes another word in the list will trigger the meaning you have forgotten. (Don't leave any space blank; try to come up with a meaning which may at least be close.)
• When studying for a vocabulary test in a special subject, try to relate words to those you already know. Look for common root words to help you.
• Don't try to study vocabulary words which are contained in the text. Make a list from the text and study the list. Even if you know a definition, write it out just for practice and as a memory aid.

CHAPTER 6

Odds and Ends

By now you know all you need to know in order to prepare for and master tests. What it all comes down to now is learning which study methods work best for you and then putting them to use. This final chapter offers some additional hints which are intended to take you just a little further toward attaining the ability to face tests with confidence.

Get Inside Your Teacher's Mind

Understanding how your teacher thinks in order to have an edge on mastering that teacher's tests is important.

Teachers are pleased when their students score well on tests. This is taken as a sign that the class is well taught and that students care enough about the material to have studied it. Though teachers may devise difficult tests, they still want their students to achieve high scores. Thus it stands to reason teachers do things intended to help their classes learn and, as a result, pass their tests. As a student out to master tests, it is worth the effort to observe and listen so you can better anticipate what will appear on upcoming tests.

The following ideas may enable you to understand your teacher's actions and thoughts regarding tests and their content.

• Teachers tend to emphasize in class those items which will appear on tests. Some repeat the same fact several times. Others note these items on the chalkboard, while many make a point of asking class members to repeat the fact or use it as an answer to a discussion question.

• Learn to listen for key words and phrases teachers use when stressing important ideas: "Put this in your notes." "This is important." "You need to remember this." "Let me repeat this." It is likely that teachers will have these items in mind later, when formulating test questions.

• We all have habits, though we may not be aware of them. Everyone has heard the jokes about the teachers who always show movies on Friday. Some teachers always schedule tests on Monday to allow their students to have the weekend for study. Others tend to have pop quizzes on Wednesday to "wake up" their classes in the middle of the week. If you can spot such habits or tendencies, it may give you an edge in understanding your teacher and his or her tests.

• Jill's history teacher never assigned the self-checking tests at the end of each chapter. One day Jill happened to glance at one of these chapter-review tests and recognized some of the questions from her teacher's previous test. From then on Jill always worked out the answers at each chapter's end because a good many of them were always on her teacher's tests. You should be so lucky!

• Is your teacher likely to play verbal tricks during class or is he or she direct and to the point? Teachers' tests are often quite like the teacher, so try to keep any eye out for such nuances.

It's important to remember not to outsmart yourself by trying to outguess your teacher. *Do* take advantage of any clues his or her actions give, but don't get carried away.

Watch for Typos

No matter how careful a test writer is, there is always the possibility of a test reaching your desk containing typographical errors. A simple typo such as misspelling "then" as "thne" doesn't affect you other than taking a second or two extra to decipher. A typo in a date is something else again. It becomes extremely important when 1901 appears as 1910 and you are asked to match the date with an event. Worst of all are typos on math tests, which are probably the most difficult to spot. Put simply, when you are asked to find the area of a field 500' by 125," you need to know whether this is a typo or a tricky question. Typos in science formulas are just as infuriating, if not more.

The only way to guard against typos is to have prepared so well that you can spot them yourself. Once spotted, call the typo to your teacher's attention to verify that it is indeed an error and not just your misreading. It goes without saying you don't want to provide the rest of the class a minute of comic relief by pointing out typos which aren't.

Keep Old Tests for Future Study Guides

"Well, that's over." Crumple, crumple, wad, wad and slam goes another returned test into the wastebasket. You've seen others do this and perhaps have fired a few such tests into the trash yourself. A far better move is to hang on to returned tests and make a test file for each class.

Previous tests are excellent study guides when midterm and final tests roll around. Depending upon the class and your teacher, it is more than likely that questions on former tests will reappear on finals. The questions may be worded differently but the content is virtually the same. If a topic is important enough to rate a test question once, it is not beyond the realm of reason to assume it may be worth a question on the final.

Even if the questions themselves don't reappear on later tests, old tests give you a quick refresher course on the sort of questions each teacher asks and the type of information a teacher expects you to recall. And at the very least, your previous tests are a great source of review questions when you begin to study for finals.

Become "Test-Wise"

Part of learning how to master tests is becoming test-wise. We have already covered much of what it takes to become a test-wise student. For instance, watching for information in one question which helps answer another question is the mark of one who is test-wise. So are remembering the tips regarding the various types of objective tests, knowing how to eliminate impossible answers and having the ability to spot an obviously false question. The truly test-wise student knows that each teacher prefers certain types of questions and tends to write tests in specific ways. A test-wise student has no trouble with key words such as *compare, contrast, explain* and *illustrate* in essay tests. In short, the test-wise student takes to heart the tips, hints and advice in this book and makes them seem as natural as exhaling or adding two plus two.

Being test-wise does not mean you will ace every test. It does give you an extra push every time you face a test. The great thing about becoming test-wise is that your test-taking ability improves with every test you take.

Know Your Strengths and Weaknesses

Throughout this book we have pointed out ways of preparing for tests which help offset your personal weaknesses. It's just as important to know your areas of strength.

• Do you tend to put off study? Then you need to set a specific time for study and stick to that schedule.

• Do you become sleepy following a big meal? If so, it is obvious you won't do your best studying immediately after dinner each evening.

• Is it difficult for you to remember all the facts you need to know for a test? Work with various mnemonic aids to find those which make memorization least difficult.

• If writing a fact helps you remember it, by all means write down those things you need to learn. Then write them again and again — as many times as you feel necessary.

• Discover what works for you and put that information to work. Just remember that a study program which is successful for one class may need to be revised to bring the same success in a different class. Don't be afraid to experiment until you find just the proper approach for each class.

• Be honest with yourself about areas in which you are weak. Denial does not solve the problem and usually makes things worse. If you can't see the chalkboard and find the text blurring, it's time to have your eyes checked or your glasses changed. If your lack of reading ability is slowing you down, seek some help in improving your reading skills.

Make the most of your strong points while working to improve those in which you are weak. Once you isolate a weakness, get to work improving that area or finding another way to study which makes up for the lack.

Now Go Out and Knock Them Dead!

You now know the basics of test mastery. It's time to put these ideas and skills to practical use.

No matter how carefully you apply the ideas in this book, every test is not going to turn into a bed of roses. Just don't let a setback or two throw you for a loop. Even though you don't get an A on every test, it doesn't mean you can't master the art of taking, passing and acing tests. If you do poorly, try to understand what happened so you don't make the same errors when you prepare for the next test.

Remember, every bit of study you do is preparation for an upcoming test. Remember, too, that tests are always just around the corner. The better you understand which study methods work for you, the better prepared you'll be for them.

Let's close with this thought: The better prepared you are, the more confident you will feel. Confidence in yourself is a major step toward mastering tests. If you just remember to be confident — not overconfident — you'll come through in fine shape.

TEST-TAKING TIPS

- Tests often reflect a teacher's personality and teaching style — so pay attention and become test-wise!
- Know your material so well you can pick out misleading typos.
- Your old tests — no matter how you did on them — are terrific study guides.
- Be honest with yourself about your strengths and weaknesses.
  Have confidence!

ANSWERS TO SELF-TESTS

☞ The multiple-choice answers are 1-e, 2-a, 3-d, 4-a and 5-e.

☞ Matching answers are 1-e, 2-a, 3-g, 4-b and 5-d.

☞ The true/false answers are 1-F, 2-F, 3-F, 4-F and 5-F. (Did it bother you that all the answers were false? Sometimes teachers will do this just to see if you get spooked and then change an answer or two to avoid having them all the same.)

☞ Completion answers are 1-objective, 2-matching (objective might get a point as well), 3-entire (whole is all right), 4- foils and 5-fill-in.

INDEX

Do term papers scare you? Are you puzzled when your teacher starts talking about character studies, plot summaries and open critiques? If you said yes to either of these questions, *Make the Grade!—Essays and Reports* will make your life a whole lot easier.

Essays and Reports will show you how you can:

- choose a subject you can live with
- make the library work for you
- put life into your reports
- reduce term-paper anxiety
- master the fine points of bibliographies and footnotes

Price Stern Sloan's
Make the Grade!—
Essays and Reports

What It Takes to Research, Write and Present an A+ Paper!